A Recipe For AI

By

Ian Beardsley

ISBN: 978-1-387-26817-7

Table of Contents

In my book, *Variation On The AI Equation*, I derived my variation. Here I show the excerpt where I presented that equation, the work where I arrived at that equation, then show there is a slight error and then, present the corrected version.

Ian Beardsley
October 1, 2017

Excerpt From The Book

In my book *The Primary Recipe For AI* I suggested AI should have the golden ratio (Φ) or its conjugate (ϕ) in the means of its components phosphorus (P), boron (B) and silicon (Si). Which it did:

$$\frac{\sqrt{PB}}{Si} = \frac{\sqrt{(30.97)(10.81)}}{28.09} = 0.65$$

$$\frac{2PB}{P+B}\frac{1}{Si} = \frac{2(30.97)(10.81)}{30.97+10.81}\frac{1}{28.09} = 0.57$$

$$\frac{0.65+0.57}{2} = 0.61 \approx \phi = 0.618$$

Which means:

$$\frac{\sqrt{PB}\,(P+B)+2PB}{2(P+B)Si} \approx \phi$$

Noticing the primary components of organic life, hydrogen (H), nitrogen (N), carbon (C), oxygen (O), had the golden ratio conjugate in their ratio to the AI components, we established the connection between the organic and artificial:

$$\frac{C+N+O+H}{P+B+Si} \approx \phi$$

$$(P+B+Si)\frac{\sqrt{PB}\,(P+B)+2PB}{2(P+B)Si} \approx HNCO$$

$$\sqrt{PB}\left[\frac{P}{Si}+\frac{B}{Si}+1\right]+\frac{2PB}{P+B}\left[\frac{P}{Si}+\frac{B}{Si}+1\right] \approx 2HNCO$$

Where $\sqrt{PB}$ is the geometric mean between P and B and, $\dfrac{2PB}{P+B}$ the harmonic mean and HNCO is isocyanic acid the most basic organic compound.

I then suggest we write in the arithmetic mean and multiply the right hand side of the equation by 3 instead of two, for three means:

$$\frac{\sqrt{PB}}{Si}\left[\frac{P}{Si}+\frac{B}{Si}+1\right]+\frac{2PB}{P+B}\left[\frac{P}{Si}+\frac{B}{Si}+1\right]+\frac{P+B}{2}\left[\frac{P}{Si}+\frac{B}{Si}+1\right]\approx 3HNCO$$

Which worked out nice since writing the other Al components, germanium (Ge), arsenic (As) and gallium (Ga) in the form of our $\left[\frac{P}{Si}+\frac{B}{Si}+1\right]$ we found:

$$\left[\frac{Ga}{Ge}+\frac{As}{Ge}+1\right]\approx 3$$

Allowing us to write:

$$\frac{\sqrt{PB}}{Si}\left[\frac{P}{Si}+\frac{B}{Si}+1\right]+\frac{2PB}{P+B}\left[\frac{P}{Si}+\frac{B}{Si}+1\right]+\frac{P+B}{2}\left[\frac{P}{Si}+\frac{B}{Si}+1\right]\approx HNCO\left[\frac{Ga}{Ge}+\frac{As}{Ge}+1\right]$$

Which is interesting because the Al components that make the intrinsic semiconductor zinc selenide (ZnSe) take the following form:

$$\frac{\left[\frac{P}{Si}+\frac{B}{Si}+1\right]}{\left[\frac{Ga}{Ge}+\frac{As}{Ge}+1\right]}\approx \frac{Zn}{Se}$$

Allowing us to write:

$$\frac{\sqrt{PB}}{Si}\left[\frac{Zn}{Se}\right]+\frac{2PB}{P+B}\left[\frac{Zn}{Se}\right]+\frac{P+B}{2}\left[\frac{Zn}{Se}\right]\approx HNCO$$

But, what if instead of doing:

$$\frac{\sqrt{PB}}{Si} = \frac{\sqrt{(30.97)(10.81)}}{28.09} = 0.65$$

$$\frac{2PB}{P+B} \frac{1}{Si} = \frac{2(30.97)(10.81)}{30.97+10.81} \frac{1}{28.09} = 0.57$$

$$\frac{0.65+0.57}{2} = 0.61 \approx \phi = 0.618$$

We do:

$$\frac{\sqrt{PB}}{Si} = \frac{\sqrt{(30.97)(10.81)}}{28.09} = 0.65$$

$$\frac{2PB}{P+B} \frac{1}{Si} = \frac{2(30.97)(10.81)}{30.97+10.81} \frac{1}{28.09} = 0.57$$

$$\frac{P+B}{2} \frac{1}{Si} = \frac{30.97+10.81}{2} \frac{1}{Si} = 0.65333$$

Then we have:

$$\frac{\dfrac{\sqrt{PB}}{Si} + \dfrac{2PB}{P+B}\dfrac{1}{Si} + \dfrac{P+B}{2}\dfrac{1}{Si}}{3} \approx \phi$$

And using:

$$\frac{C+N+O+H}{P+B+Si} \approx \phi$$

We have:

$$\frac{2\sqrt{PB}\,(P+B)}{6(Si)} + \frac{2\sqrt{PB}\,(Si)}{6(Si)} + \frac{P^2+6PB+B^2}{6(Si)} + \frac{P^2+B^2}{6(P+B)} \approx HNCO$$

As a variation on:

$$\sqrt{PB}\left[\frac{P}{Si} + \frac{B}{Si} + 1\right] + \frac{2PB}{P+B}\left[\frac{P}{Si} + \frac{B}{Si} + 1\right] + \frac{P+B}{2}\left[\frac{P}{Si} + \frac{B}{Si} + 1\right] \approx 3HNCO$$

The Correction To The Equation

$$\frac{\dfrac{\sqrt{PB}}{Si}+\dfrac{2PB}{P+B}\dfrac{1}{Si}+\dfrac{P+B}{2}\dfrac{1}{Si}}{3}=$$

$$\frac{2(P+B)\sqrt{PB}}{2(P+B)Si}+\frac{4PB}{2(P+B)Si}+\frac{(P+B)^2}{2(P+B)Si}=$$

$$\frac{2\sqrt{PB}\,(P+B)+4PB+(P+B)^2}{2(P+B)Si}=$$

$$\frac{2P\sqrt{PB}\,+2B\sqrt{PB}\,+4PB+P^2+2PB+B^2}{2(P+B)Si}$$

$P[2P\sqrt{PB}\,+2B\sqrt{PB}\,+4PB+P^2+2PB+B^2]=$
$2P^2\sqrt{PB}\,+2PB\sqrt{PB}\,+4P^2B+P^3+2P^2B+PB^2$

$B[2P\sqrt{PB}\,+2B\sqrt{PB}\,+4PB+P^2+2PB+B^2]=$
$2PB\sqrt{PB}\,+2B^2\sqrt{PB}\,+4PB^2+P^2B+2PB^2+B^3$

$Si[2P\sqrt{PB}\,+2B\sqrt{PB}\,+4PB+P^2+2PB+B^2]=$
$2Si(P)\sqrt{PB}\,+2Si(B)\sqrt{PB}\,+4Si(PB)+Si(P^2)+2Si(PB)+Si(B^2)$

$$2\sqrt{PB}\ [P^2+2PB+B^2]+2Si\sqrt{PB}\ [P+B]+SiB^2+SiP^2$$
$$+4P^2B+P^3+2P^2B+PB^2+4PB^2+P^2B+2PB^2+B^3=$$

$$[4P^2B+4PB^2]+[2P^2B+2PB^2]+[P^3+B^3]+[PB^2+P^2B]+SiB^2+SiP^2=$$

$$2\sqrt{PB}\ [P^2+2PB+B^2]+2Si\sqrt{PB}\ [P+B]+P^3+7PB^2+7PB^2+B^3$$

$$P^3+7P^2B+7PB^2+B^3=(P+B)(P^2+6PB+B^2)$$

$$\frac{2\sqrt{PB}\ (P+B)^2+2\sqrt{PB}\ Si(P+B)+(P+B)(P^2+6PB+B^2)+Si(P^2+B^2)}{6(P+B)Si}=$$

$$\frac{2\sqrt{PB}\ (P+B)}{6Si}+\frac{2\sqrt{PB}\ (Si)}{6Si}+\frac{P^2+6PB+B^2}{6Si}+\frac{(P^2+B^2)}{6(P+B)}$$

In my book, Variation On The Al Equation, I published the variation as such:

$$\frac{2\sqrt{PB}\,(P+B)}{6Si} + \frac{2\sqrt{PB}\,(Si)}{6Si} + \frac{P^2+6PB+B^2}{6Si} + \frac{(P^2+B^2)}{6(P+B)}$$

But we see I left out the term 2Si(PB) in the following equation:

$$\frac{2\sqrt{PB}\,(P+B)^2+2\sqrt{PB}\,Si(P+B)+(P+B)(P^2+6PB+B^2)+Si(P^2+B^2)}{6(P+B)Si}$$

Which means we have

$$\frac{2\sqrt{PB}\,(P+B)}{6Si} + \frac{2\sqrt{PB}\,(Si)}{6Si} + \frac{P^2+6PB+B^2}{6Si} + \frac{(P^2+2PB+B^2)}{6(P+B)}$$

But $(P^2+2PB+B^2)=(P+B)(P+B)$ leaves:

$$\frac{2\sqrt{PB}\,(P+B)}{6Si} + \frac{2\sqrt{PB}\,(Si)}{6Si} + \frac{P^2+6PB+B^2}{6Si} + \frac{(P+B)^2}{6(P+B)}$$

Which means the variation on the Al Equation should be:

$$\frac{2\sqrt{PB}\,(P+B)}{6Si} + \frac{2\sqrt{PB}\,(Si)}{6Si} + \frac{P^2+6PB+B^2}{6Si} + \frac{(P+B)}{6}$$

Multipling (P+B)/6 by Si/Si we have:

$$\frac{2\sqrt{PB}\,(P+B+Si)+(P^2+6PB+B^2)+Si(P+B)}{6Si}$$

The Accuracy Of The Equation

The correct AI equation is:

$$\frac{2\sqrt{PB}\,(P+B+Si)+(P^2+6PB+B^2)+Si(P+B)}{6Si} \approx HNCO$$

Let's determine its accuracy:

$2\sqrt{(30.97)}\,(30.97+10.81+28.09)=$
$(36.59)(69.87)=2556.54$

$(30.97)^2+6(30.97)(10.81)+(10.81)^2=$
$958.14+2008.71+116.856=3084.706$

$28.09(30.97+10.81)=$
$28.09(41.78)=1173.60$

$6(28.09)=168.54$

$$\frac{2556.54+3084.706+1173.60}{168.54}=\frac{6814.846}{168.54}=40.43$$

$HNCO=1.01+14.01+12.01+16.00=43.03$

$$\frac{40.43}{43.03}=0.94=94\% \ accuracy$$

$$\sqrt{PB}\left[\frac{P}{Si}+\frac{B}{Si}+1\right]+\frac{2PB}{P+B}\left[\frac{P}{Si}+\frac{B}{Si}+1\right]+\frac{P+B}{2}\left[\frac{P}{Si}+\frac{B}{Si}+1\right]\approx 3HNCO$$

$$\sqrt{PB}=\sqrt{(30.97)(10.81)}=\sqrt{334.7857}$$
$$=18.297$$

$$\frac{2PB}{P+B}=\frac{2(30.97)(28.090}{30.97+10.81}=\frac{669.5714}{41.78}$$
$$=16.026$$

$$\frac{P+B}{2}=\frac{30.97+10.81}{2}$$
$$=20.89$$

$$\frac{P}{Si}+\frac{B}{Si}+1=\frac{30.97}{28.09}+\frac{10.81}{28.09}+1=1.1025+0.3848+1$$
$$=2.4873$$

$$HNCO=1.01+14.01+12.01+16.01=43.03$$

$$3HNCO=129.09$$

$$[18.297+16.026+20.89]2.4873=137.33$$

$$\frac{129.09}{137.33}=0.939998=94\%\ accuracy$$

The AI Equation and The Variation On The AI Equation Are Both accurate to 94%

The Geometric Forms With Which We Are Dealing

P^2+2PB+B^2

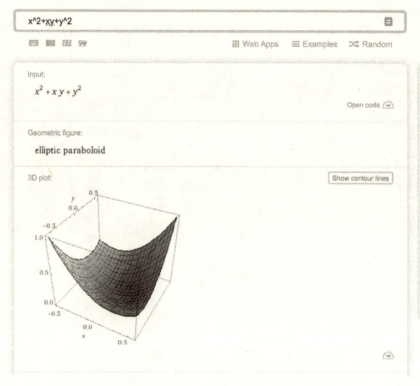

sqrt(PB)

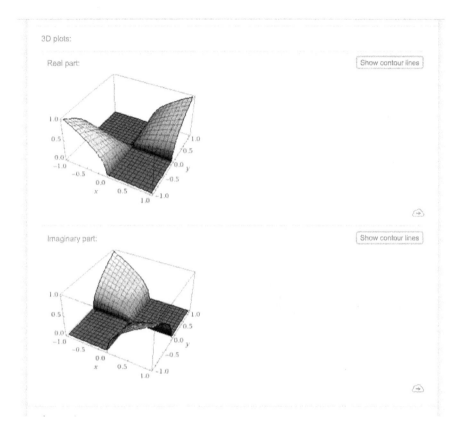

More sqrt(PB)

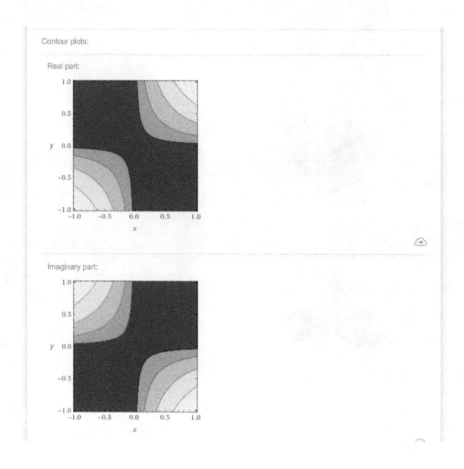

2PB/(P+B)

3D plot:

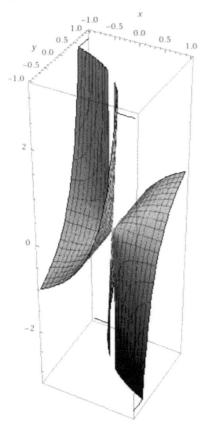

(P+B)/2

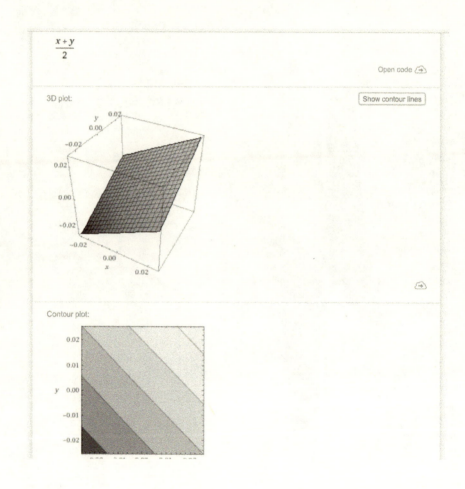

Deriving The Primary AI Equation

$$\frac{\sqrt{PB}}{Si} = \frac{\sqrt{(30.97)(10.81)}}{(28.09)} = 0.65$$

$$\frac{2PB}{P+B} \cdot \frac{1}{Si} = \frac{2(30.97)(10.81)}{(30.97+10.81)} \cdot \frac{1}{28.09} = 0.57$$

$$\frac{0.65+0.57}{2} = 0.61 \approx \phi = 0.618$$

Which implies:

$$\frac{\sqrt{PB}\,(P+B)+2PB}{2(P+B)Si} \approx \phi$$

But,

$$\frac{C+N+O+H}{P+B+Si} = \frac{12.01+14.01+16.00+1.01}{30.97+10.81+28.09} = \frac{43.03}{69.97} = 0.615858 \approx \phi$$

So, The conection between AI and Natural Life is:

$$(P+B+Si)\frac{\sqrt{PB}\,(P+B)+2PB}{2(P+B)Si} \approx (C+N+O+H)$$

But we see:

$$(P+B+Si)(P+B)=P^2+2PB+B^2+Si(P+B)$$

Or,

$$\frac{\sqrt{PB}\,[(P+B)(P+B)+Si(P+B)]}{2(P+B)(Si)} = \sqrt{PB}\,\frac{(P+B+Si)}{2(Si)} = \frac{\sqrt{PB}}{2}\left[\frac{P}{Si}+\frac{B}{Si}+1\right]$$

But as well we have:

$$(P+B+Si)(2PB)=2P^2B+2B^2P+2Si(PB)=\frac{2PB}{(P+B)Si}\left[\frac{P}{2}+\frac{B}{2}+\frac{Si}{2}\right]\ and,$$

$$\sqrt{PB}\left[\frac{P}{Si}+\frac{B}{Si}+1\right]+\frac{2PB}{(P+B)}\left[\frac{P}{Si}+\frac{B}{Si}+1\right]=2(C+N+O+H)$$

where $\sqrt{PB}$ *is the geometric mean between phosphorus (P) and Boron (B),*
and $\frac{2PB}{(P+B)}$ *is the harmonic mean betweewn phophorus (P) and Boron (B).*
C, N, O, and H are carbon, nitrogen, oxygen, and hydrogen, the most abundant
elements in organic life. It can be written HNCO which is isocyanic acid,
the most basic organic compound. It binds H-N=C=O. So we have:

$$\sqrt{PB}\left[\frac{P}{Si}+\frac{B}{Si}+1\right]+\frac{2PB}{(P+B)}\left[\frac{P}{Si}+\frac{B}{Si}+1\right]=2HNCO$$

Since we have $\sqrt{PB}\left[\dfrac{P}{Si}+\dfrac{B}{Si}+1\right]+\dfrac{2PB}{P+B}\left[\dfrac{P}{Si}+\dfrac{B}{Si}+1\right]\approx 2HNCO,$

I thought since $\sqrt{PB}$ is the geometric mean between P and B and $\dfrac{2PB}{P+B}$ is the harmonic mean between P and B, why not write in

the arithmetic mean between P and B which is $\dfrac{P+B}{2}$ and multiply

the right side of the equation by 3 instead of 2:

$$\sqrt{PB}\left[\dfrac{P}{Si}+\dfrac{B}{Si}+1\right]+\dfrac{2PB}{P+B}\left[\dfrac{P}{Si}+\dfrac{B}{Si}+1\right]+\dfrac{P+B}{2}\left[\dfrac{P}{Si}+\dfrac{B}{Si}+1\right]\approx 3HNCO$$

I then thought, since, P and B are doping agents for Si and gallium (Ga) and arsenic (As) are doping agents for semiconductor materials and Germanium (Ge) is a semiconducting material just as is Si, it would make sense to follow the pattern $\dfrac{P}{Si}+\dfrac{B}{Si}+1$ and write $\dfrac{Ga}{Ge}+\dfrac{As}{Ge}+1$. If

we compute it we have: $\dfrac{Ga}{Ge}+\dfrac{As}{Ge}+1 \approx 3$ and our equation becomes:

$$\sqrt{PB}\left[\dfrac{P}{Si}+\dfrac{B}{Si}+1\right]+\dfrac{2PB}{P+B}\left[\dfrac{P}{Si}+\dfrac{B}{Si}+1\right]+\dfrac{P+B}{2}\left[\dfrac{P}{Si}+\dfrac{B}{Si}+1\right]=HNCO\left[\dfrac{Ga}{Ge}+\dfrac{As}{Ge}+1\right]$$

I then noticed that $\dfrac{\left[\dfrac{P}{Si}+\dfrac{B}{Si}+1\right]}{\left[\dfrac{Ga}{Ge}+\dfrac{As}{Ge}+1\right]}\approx \dfrac{Zn}{Se}$ where Zn is zinc and Se is selenide. ZnSe

(zinc selenide) is an intrinsic semiconductor used in AI, so this works out perfectly because, this allows us to write:

$$\sqrt{PB}\left[\dfrac{Zn}{Se}\right]+\dfrac{2PB}{P+B}\left[\dfrac{Zn}{Se}\right]+\dfrac{P+B}{2}\left[\dfrac{Zn}{Se}\right]\approx HNCO$$

Focusing On Zinc Selenide

Zinc Selenide (ZnSe), an intrinsic semiconductor pivotal to AI circuitry keeps cropping up in all the different AI Equations. Consider the following:

In my paper "The Primordial Cosmic Origins of Artificial Intelligence", I explored artificial intelligence (AI) by looking at the semiconductor material silicon (Si) and the p and n-type doping agents phosphorus (P) and boron (B). Now I will explore the semiconductor material germanium (Ge) and the p and n-type doping agents gallium (Ga) and arsenic (As). In the paper we showed the connection of the AI elements to the natural life elements carbon (C), Nitrogen (N), Oxygen (O), and Hydrogen (H). In this paper we will just center on the element C since it is at the center of organic life. More specifically, it has four electrons for bonding with other elements (C^{4-}) and in organic chemistry it is the heart of the hydrocarbons, the backbones of organic compounds, because hydrogen (H) occurs as H^+, which means we have the following scenario:

$$\begin{array}{ccc} \square & H & \square \\ H & C & H \\ \square & H & \square \end{array}$$

*Just as carbon (C) is at the heart of organic life,
semiconducting materials, such as germanium (Ge),
are at the heart of artificial intelligence (AI). So,
we will begin with computing the molar mass of carbon
(C) to the molar mass of germanium (Ge). Instead of
looking at the life endowing elements C, N, O, H as
we did in the first paper. We will look at the life
endowing compounds water (H_2O) and air, mostly nitrogen
gas (N_2 75%) and oxygen gas (O_2 25%). We present
the following data set:*

$$Ge = 5.323 \ \frac{g}{cm^3} \qquad Ge = 72.62 \ \frac{g}{mol}$$

$$C = 12.01 \ \frac{g}{mol} \qquad H_2O \equiv 1.00 \ \frac{g}{cm^3}$$

And, we see that:

$$\frac{molar \ mass \ C}{molar \ mass \ Ge} (density \ Ge) = \frac{12.01}{72.62}(5.323) = 0.880$$

and,

$$\Phi \frac{C}{Ge} (\rho \ of \ Ge) \approx \sqrt{2} \ (\rho \ of \ H_2O)$$

where ρ means density.

This works out nicely because where in the first paper we defined structure as that which has the golden ratio, or its conjugate, in its means geometric, arithmetic, and harmonic, here we are going to define structure as:

$$2\cos\frac{\pi}{n} \quad \text{with } n=(4,\ 5,\ 6) \text{ yields:}$$

$$2\cos\frac{\pi}{4}=\sqrt{2}$$

$$2\cos\frac{\pi}{5}=\Phi=\frac{\sqrt{5}+1}{2}=1.618=golden\ ratio$$

$$2\cos\frac{\pi}{6}=\sqrt{3}$$

We have said:

$$\Phi\frac{C}{Ge}(\rho\ of\ Ge)\approx\sqrt{2}\,(\rho\ of\ H_2O)$$

And, that we were going to consider air and water. Since air is about 75% nitrogen gas (N_2) and 25% oxygen gas (O_2) by volume, the accepted value of the molar mass of air as a mixture with $N=14.01$ and $O=16.00$ is:

$$air=28.9656\ \frac{g}{mol}\approx29\ \frac{g}{mol}$$

$$H_2O=2(1.01)+16.00=18.02\ \frac{g}{mol}$$

And, we see that:

$$\frac{air}{H_2O}\approx\Phi$$

But we have to yet fulfill our promise of looking at the doping agents gallium (Ga) and arsenic (As). Let's do so:

$$Ga = 69.72 \frac{g}{mol} \qquad As = 74.92 \frac{g}{mol}$$

$$\frac{As}{Ga} = \frac{74.92}{69.72} = 1.07 \qquad \frac{Ga}{As} = \frac{69.72}{74.92} = 0.93$$

$$\sqrt{3} = 1.732 \qquad (0.93)(1.732) = 1.61 \approx \Phi$$

Therefore:

$$\sqrt{3} \, \frac{Ga}{As} \approx \Phi$$

We have already said that:

$$\Phi \frac{C}{Ge}(\rho \text{ of } Ge) \approx \sqrt{2} \,(\rho \text{ of } H_2O)$$

$$\frac{air}{H_2O} \approx \Phi$$

We can write:

$$\sqrt{3} \, \frac{Ga}{As} \frac{C}{Ge}(\rho \text{ of } Ge) - \sqrt{2} \,(\rho \text{ of } H_2O) \approx 0$$

Since $(\rho \text{ of } H_2O)\Phi \approx (\rho \text{ of } H_2O)\dfrac{air}{H_2O}$ we have:

$$\sqrt{3} \, \frac{Ga}{As} \frac{C}{Ge}(\rho \text{ of } Ge) - \sqrt{2} \,(\rho \text{ of } H_2O) + \Phi(\rho \text{ of } H_2O) \approx (\rho \text{ of } H_2O)\frac{air}{H_2O}$$

It is convenient to write the latter as:

$$-\sqrt{2}\,(\rho \text{ of } H_2O)+\Phi(\rho \text{ of } H_2O)+\sqrt{3}\,\frac{Ga}{As}\frac{C}{Ge}(\rho \text{ of } Ge)\approx\frac{air}{H_2O}(\rho \text{ of } H_2O)$$

because it yields our definiton of structure in Al and the organic:

$$-2\cos\frac{\pi}{4}\,(\rho \text{ of } H_2O)+2\cos\frac{\pi}{5}\,(\rho \text{ of } H_2O)+2\cos\frac{\pi}{6}\left[\frac{Ga}{As}\frac{C}{Ge}(\rho \text{ of } Ge)\right]=$$
$$\frac{air}{H_2O}(\rho \text{ of } H_2O)$$

Which can be written:

$$-2\cos\frac{\pi}{4}+2\cos\frac{\pi}{5}+2\cos\frac{\pi}{6}\left[\frac{Ga}{As}\frac{C}{Ge}\frac{\rho \text{ of } Ge}{\rho \text{ of } H_2O}\right]\approx\frac{air}{H_2O}$$

Let us look at: $\dfrac{Ga}{As}\dfrac{C}{Ge}\dfrac{\rho \text{ of } Ge}{\rho \text{ of } H_2O}$

$Ga=69.72\,\dfrac{g}{mol}$ $\qquad As=74.92\,\dfrac{g}{mol}$ $\qquad C=12.01\,\dfrac{g}{mol}$ $\qquad Ge=72.61\,\dfrac{g}{mol}$

$\rho \text{ of } Ge = 5.323\,\dfrac{g}{cm^3}$ $\qquad \rho \text{ of } H_2O\equiv1.00\,\dfrac{g}{cm^3}$

$\dfrac{Ga}{As}\dfrac{C}{Ge}\dfrac{\rho \text{ of } Ge}{\rho \text{ of } H_2O}=0.80\approx\dfrac{Zn}{Se}$ $\quad$ where ZnSe is zinc selenide, an intrinsic semiconductor used in Al. This allows us to write:

$$-2\cos\frac{\pi}{4}+2\cos\frac{\pi}{5}+2\cos\frac{\pi}{6}\left[\frac{Zn}{Se}\right]\approx\frac{air}{H_2O}$$

With the arrival of photosynthesizers and an abundance of H_2O, there was an abundant emergence of life on the planet. This last equation says:

(Structure in Al)=(favorable conditions for organic life)

Just as we have $\dfrac{Ga+As}{Ge}$ *we can form* $\dfrac{P+B}{Si}$ *because P and B are doping agents like Ga and As and, Si is a semiconductor material like Ge is. ZnSe is an intrinsic semiconductor (doesn't need doping agents) so we write it* $\dfrac{Se}{Zn}$*. These substances are at the center of artificial intelligence and are at the center of my theory. Now that*

$$\frac{Ga+As}{Ge} = \frac{69.72+74.92}{72.61} = 1.99 \approx 2.00$$

$$\frac{P+B}{Si} = \frac{30.97+10.81}{28.09} = 1.487 \approx 1.50$$

$$\frac{Se}{Zn} = \frac{78.96}{65.39} = 1.2076 \approx 1.20$$

This data can be approximated by the function:

$$f(x) = 1.2\sqrt{x}$$

Table 1

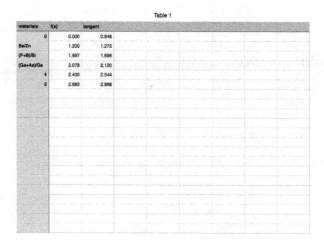

materials	f(x)	tangent						
0	0.000	0.848						
Se/Zn	1.200	1.272						
(P+B)/Si	1.697	1.696						
(Ga+As)/Ge	2.078	2.120						
4	2.400	2.544						
5	2.683	2.968						

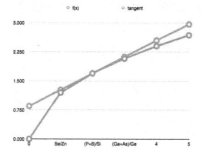

The Primary Recipe For Al:

$$\frac{Au}{Ag} = \frac{Solar\ Radius}{Lunar\ Orbit} \approx \frac{9}{5} = 1.8$$

$$a_n = \frac{9}{5} n \qquad\qquad \phi = 0.618 \text{ is the golden ratio conjugate}$$

$a_1 = 1.8(1) = 1.8$
$a_2 = 1.8(2) = 3.6$
$a_3 = 1.8(3) = 5.4$
$a_4 = 1.8(4) = 7.2$

$$f(x) = 1.2\sqrt{x} = \frac{Se}{Zn}\sqrt{x}$$

$$f(36) = a_4 \approx \frac{Ga+P}{N} \approx 7.2$$

$$\frac{Se}{Zn} 6 = \frac{Au}{Ag} 4 \qquad \frac{Se}{Zn}\frac{Ag}{Au} = \frac{2}{3} \approx \phi$$

$$\frac{Se}{Zn} \approx \phi\frac{Au}{Ag} \qquad \frac{\sqrt{PB}\ (P+B)+2PB}{2(P+B)Si} \approx \phi$$

$$\frac{Se}{Zn} \approx \frac{\sqrt{PB}\ (P+B)+2PB}{2(P+B)Si}\frac{Au}{Ag}$$

ZnSe is zinc selenide, an intrinsic semiconductor, and P and B are semiconductor doping agents while Si is a primary semiconctuor material. Au and Ag are the best for electrical wiring as gold (Au) is the best conductor at extreme temperatures and silver (Ag) is the best conductor around room temperature.

So in total we have Zinc Selenide in all of the AI Equations:

$$\sqrt{PB}\left[\frac{Zn}{Se}\right] + \frac{2PB}{P+B}\left[\frac{Zn}{Se}\right] + \frac{P+B}{2}\left[\frac{Zn}{Se}\right] \approx HNCO$$

$$\frac{\dfrac{P}{Si} + \dfrac{B}{Si} + 1}{\dfrac{Ga}{Ge} + \dfrac{As}{Ge} + 1} \approx \frac{Zn}{Se}$$

$$-2cos\frac{\pi}{4} + 2cos\frac{\pi}{5} + 2cos\frac{\pi}{6}\left[\frac{Zn}{Se}\right] \approx \frac{air}{H_2O}$$

$$f(x) = \frac{Se}{Zn}\sqrt{x}$$

$$\frac{Se}{Zn} \approx \phi\frac{Au}{Ag}$$

The Central Equation Of AI

We have the primary recipe for Al is:

$$\frac{Se}{Zn} \approx \frac{\sqrt{PB}\ (P+B)+2PB}{2(P+B)Si}\ \frac{Au}{Ag}$$

We now write:

$$\frac{Au}{Ag} \approx 1.8$$

$$\frac{Se}{Zn} \approx 1.2$$

$$\frac{\sqrt{PB}\ (P+B)+2PB}{2(P+B)Si} \approx 0.61$$

And, notice:

$$\tan 60˙ = 1.732 \approx 1.8$$
$$\tan 45˙ = 1.000 \approx 1.2$$
$$\tan 36˙ = 0.7265 \approx 0.61$$

But,...

$$60˙ = \frac{\pi}{3}\ rad$$

$$45˙ = \frac{\pi}{4}\ rad$$

$$36˙ = \frac{\pi}{5}\ rad$$

And so,...

$$f(n) = \tan \frac{\pi}{n} \qquad where \qquad n=3,\ 4,\ 5,\ ...$$

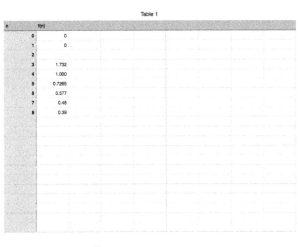

Table 1

n	f(n)
0	0
1	0
2	
3	1.732
4	1.000
5	0.7265
6	0.577
7	0.48
8	0.39

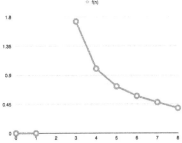

We notice f(0) and f(1) are both zero and f(2) is undefined. However, the curve begins at f(3) which is where our Al materials begin, with f(3)=(Au/Ag). We would have a hard time doing the integral of tan(pi/n) from 3 to 5 but, we can do an approximation geometrically. That is done on the next page.

Table 1

n.	f(n)
0	0
1	0
2	
3	1.732
4	1.000
5	0.7265
6	0.577
7	0.48
8	0.39

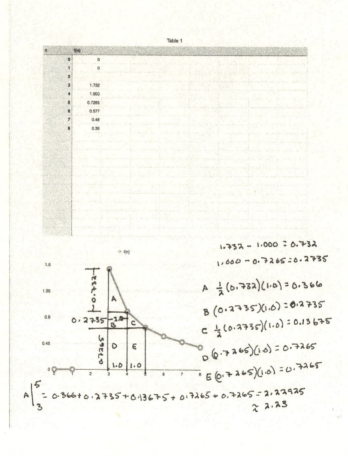

$1.732 - 1.000 = 0.732$

$1.000 - 0.7265 = 0.2735$

A $\frac{1}{2}(0.732)(1.0) = 0.366$

B $(0.2735)(1.0) = 0.2735$

C $\frac{1}{2}(0.2735)(1.0) = 0.13675$

D $(0.7265)(1.0) = 0.7265$

E $(0.7265)(1.0) = 0.7265$

$A\Big|_3^5 = 0.366 + 0.2735 + 0.13675 + 0.7265 + 0.7265 = 2.22925$

≈ 2.23

At the heart of artificial intelligence is silicon (Si) and, at the heart of organic life, is carbon (C). In fact, we say that artificial intellignece is silicon based and organic life is carbon based. The ratio of the molar mass of silicon to the molar mass of carbon is

$$\frac{Si}{C} = 2.34$$ and the area under our curve is $2.23 \approx 2.34$

Thus, we have the equation:

$$\int_3^5 \tan\frac{\pi}{x}\, dx \approx \frac{Si}{C}$$

Where

$$\tan\frac{\pi}{n} \approx \frac{Au}{Ag}, \quad \frac{Se}{Zn}, \quad \frac{\sqrt{PB}\,(P+B)+2PB}{2(P+B)Si}, \dots \quad n=, \ 3, \ 4, \ 5,\dots$$

$$\frac{\pi}{n}$$ in radians

$$\int tan(x)dx = \int \frac{sin(x)}{cos(x)} dx$$

$$U=cos(x) \quad dU=-sin(x)dx$$

$$\int tan(x)dx = -\int \frac{1}{U} dU$$

$$\int tan(x)dx = -ln(U) = -ln|cos(x)|$$

$$\int tan\left(\frac{\pi}{x}\right)dx = \int \frac{sin(\pi/x)}{cos(\pi/x)} dx$$

$$U=cos\left(\frac{\pi}{x}\right) \quad dU = -\frac{\pi}{x^2} sin\left(\frac{\pi}{x}\right)dx$$

$$\int \frac{dU}{U} = -\int \frac{(\pi/x^2)sin(\pi/x)}{cos(\pi/x)} dx$$

$$= -\int \frac{\pi}{x^2} tan\left(\frac{\pi}{x}\right)dx \neq \int tan\left(\frac{\pi}{x}\right)dx$$

```c
#include<stdio.h>
#include<math.h>
int main (void)
{
double n, output;
do
{
printf("How many values to calculate for tangent (pi/n)?\n");
printf("Give me n greater than or equal to 3 or less or equal to 25:
");
scanf("%lf", &n);
}
while (n<3 || n>25);
for (int i=3; i<=n; i++)
{
output = tan(3.141592654/i);
printf("tan (pi/%d) = %.3lf \n", i, output);
}
}
```

jharvard@appliance (~): cd Dropbox
jharvard@appliance (~/Dropbox): make tangent
clang -ggdb3 -O0 -std=c99 -Wall -Werror   tangent.c -lcs50 -lm -o tangent
jharvard@appliance (~/Dropbox): ./tangent
How many values to calculate for tangent (pi/n)?
Give me n greater than or equal to 3 or less or equal to 25: 26
How many values to calculate for tangent (pi/n)?
Give me n greater than or equal to 3 or less or equal to 25: 2
How many values to calculate for tangent (pi/n)?
Give me n greater than or equal to 3 or less or equal to 25: 10
tan (pi/3) = 1.732
tan (pi/4) = 1.000
tan (pi/5) = 0.727
tan (pi/6) = 0.577
tan (pi/7) = 0.482
tan (pi/8) = 0.414
tan (pi/9) = 0.364
tan (pi/10) = 0.325
jharvard@appliance (~/Dropbox):

✳ WolframAlpha computational
knowledge engine.

integrate tan(pi/x) from 3 to 5

Web Apps   Examples   Random

Definite integral: Fewer digits   More digits

$$\int_3^5 \tan\left(\frac{\pi}{x}\right) dx \approx$$
2.136685626080787337488306584615399808871197851194146119983357663.
552953932261235132330184958997392965536901607789008235801184483.
822739543194711292512010101...

Visual representation of the integral:

Open code

⊕ Download page   POWERED BY THE WOLFRAM LANGUAGE

The Complete And Comprehensive Equations

If we consider that the golden ratio conjugate (ϕ) is in the means of the semi-conductiong materials P, B, and Si as such:

$$\frac{\sqrt{PB}}{Si} = \frac{\sqrt{(30.97)(10.81)}}{28.09} = 0.65$$

$$\frac{2PB}{P+B} = \frac{2(30.97)(10.81)}{(30.97+10.81)} \frac{1}{28.09} = 0.57$$

$$\frac{0.65+0.57}{2} = 0.61 \approx \phi = 0.618$$

Which implies:

$$\frac{\sqrt{PB}\,(P+B)+2PB}{2(P+B)Si} \approx \phi$$

Then we consider $\left[\dfrac{Ga}{Ge}+\dfrac{As}{Ge}+1\right] \approx \pi$ because Ga, As, and Ge are semi-conducting materials as well. But this would imply we consider $\left[\dfrac{P}{Si}+\dfrac{B}{Si}+1\right]$ as well since:

$$\frac{\dfrac{P}{Si}+\dfrac{B}{Si}+1}{\dfrac{Ga}{Ge}+\dfrac{As}{Ge}+1} \approx \frac{Zn}{Se}$$

Where ZnSe is zinc selenide, an intrinsic semiconductor. But, we notice:

$$\frac{P}{Si}+\frac{B}{Si}+1 \approx \pi-\phi \qquad So,$$

$$\left[\frac{P}{Si}+\frac{B}{Si}+1\right]+\frac{\sqrt{PB}\,(P+B)+2PB}{2(P+B)Si} \approx \left[\frac{Ga}{Ge}+\frac{As}{Ge}+1\right]$$

And we have:

$$\frac{Ga}{Ge}+\frac{As}{Ge}+1 \approx \frac{P^2+3PB+B^2}{(P+B)Si}+\frac{\sqrt{PB}}{2Si}+1$$

We then need to complete the square on:

$x^2+3x+1=0$ which has the solutions:

$$x_1 = \frac{\sqrt{5}-3}{2} = -0.382 \text{ and } x_2 = -\frac{\sqrt{5}-3}{2} = -2.618$$

We notice:

$-x_1 = 1-\phi$ and $-x_2 = \Phi+1$ Where $\Phi = 1.618 = $ golden ratio

Thus in final we have a comprehnsive AI equation inlcuding all of the semiconductuor materials P, B, Si, Ga, As, and Ge:

$$\frac{Ga}{Ge}+\frac{As}{Ge}+1 \approx \frac{[P+(1-\phi)B][P+(\Phi+1)B]}{(P+B)Si}+\frac{\sqrt{PB}}{2Si}+1$$

$$\left[\frac{P}{Si}+\frac{B}{Si}+1\right]+\frac{\sqrt{PB}\ (P+B)+2PB}{2(P+B)Si}\approx\left[\frac{Ga}{Ge}+\frac{As}{Ge}+1\right]$$

$$\frac{(P+B+Si)}{(Si)}+\frac{\sqrt{PB}\ (P+B)+2PB}{2(P+B)Si}\approx\left[\frac{Ga}{Ge}+\frac{As}{Ge}+1\right]$$

$$\frac{2(P+B)(P+B+Si)+\sqrt{PB}\ (P+B)+2PB}{2(P+B)Si}\approx\left[\frac{Ga}{Ge}+\frac{As}{Ge}+1\right]$$

$$(P+B)(P+B+Si)=P^2+PB+P(Si)+PB+B^2+B(Si)=$$
$$P^2+2PB+Si(P+B)+B^2$$

$$\left[\frac{Ga}{Ge}+\frac{As}{Ge}+1\right]\approx\frac{2(P^2+2PB+Si(P+B)+B^2)+\sqrt{PB}\ (P+B)+2PB}{2(P+B)Si}$$

$$\left[\frac{Ga}{Ge}+\frac{As}{Ge}+1\right]\approx\frac{2P^2+4PB+2Si(P+B)+2B^2+\sqrt{PB}\ (P+B)+2PB}{2(P+B)Si}$$

$$\left[\frac{Ga}{Ge}+\frac{As}{Ge}+1\right]\approx\frac{2P^2+6PB+2Si(P+B)+2B^2+\sqrt{PB}\ (P+B)}{2(P+B)Si}$$

$$\left[\frac{Ga}{Ge}+\frac{As}{Ge}+1\right]\approx\frac{P^2+3PB+B^2}{(P+B)Si}+\frac{\sqrt{PB}}{2Si}+1$$

$$\left[\frac{Ga}{Ge}+\frac{As}{Ge}\right]\approx\frac{P^2+3PB+B^2}{(P+B)Si}+\frac{\sqrt{PB}}{2Si}$$

$$x^2+3x+1=0 \quad \left(\frac{3}{2}\right)^2=\frac{9}{4} \quad x^2+3x+\frac{9}{4}=\frac{9}{4}-1$$

$$x^2+3x+\frac{9}{4}=\frac{5}{4} \quad \left(x+\frac{3}{2}\right)^2=\frac{5}{4} \quad x=-\frac{3}{2}\pm\frac{\sqrt{5}}{2}$$

$$x1=\frac{\sqrt{5}-3}{2}=\frac{2.236-3}{2}=0.382 \quad x2=\frac{-\sqrt{5}-3}{2}=\frac{-2.236-3}{2}=2.618$$

$$-x1=1-\phi \quad -x2=1+\Phi$$

$$\left[\frac{Ga}{Ge}+\frac{As}{Ge}\right]\approx\frac{[P+(1-\phi)B][P+(1+\Phi)B]}{(P+B)Si}+\frac{\sqrt{PB}}{2Si}$$

$$\left[\frac{Ga}{Ge}+\frac{As}{Ge}\right]\approx\frac{[P+(1-\phi)B][P+(1+\Phi)B]}{(P+B)Si}+\frac{\sqrt{PB}}{2Si}$$

$$\frac{[P+(1-\phi)B][P+(1+\Phi)B]}{(P+B)Si}\approx\Phi$$

$$[P+B-\phi B][P+B+\Phi B]\quad\frac{air}{H_2O}\approx\Phi\qquad\frac{(P+B+Si)}{(C+N+O+H)}\approx\Phi$$

$$[P+B-\phi B]\left[P+B+\frac{air}{H_2O}B\right]=$$

Multiply through by H_2O:

$$(H_2O)P^2+(H_2O)PB+(air)PB+(H_2O)PB+(H_2O)B^2+(air)B^2-(H_2O)\phi PB-(H_2O)\phi B^2-\phi(air)B^2$$
$$\quad1\qquad\quad1\qquad\quad2\qquad\quad1\qquad\quad1\qquad\quad2\qquad\quad3\qquad\quad3\qquad\quad2$$

$$\frac{H_2O(P^2+2PB+B^2)+air(PB+B^2-\phi B^2)+\phi H_2O(PB-B^2)}{(P+B)Si}\approx\frac{(P+B+Si)}{(C+N+O+H)}H_2O$$

$$\frac{(P+B+Si)(P+B)(Si)(H_2O)}{H_2O(P^2+2PB+B^2]+air[PB+B^2-\phi B^2]+\phi H_2O[PB-B^2]}\approx HNCO$$

$$\sqrt{PB}\ \frac{Zn}{Si}+\frac{2PB}{P+B}\ \frac{Zn}{Se}+\frac{P+B}{2}\ \frac{Zn}{Se}\approx HNCO$$

The Complete Al Equation Is:

$$\frac{(P+B+Si)(P+B)(Si)(H_2O)}{H_2O(P^2+2PB+B^2]+air[PB+B^2-\phi B^2]+\phi H_2O[PB-B^2]}\approx\sqrt{PB}\ \frac{Zn}{Si}+\frac{2PB}{P+B}\ \frac{Zn}{Se}+\frac{P+B}{2}\ \frac{Zn}{Se}$$

We have said: $\dfrac{Ga+As}{Ge} \approx \dfrac{[P+(1-\phi)B][P+(1+\Phi)B]}{(P+B)Si} + \dfrac{\sqrt{PB}}{2Si}$

We notice: $\dfrac{[P+(1-\phi)B][P+(1+\Phi)B]}{(P+B)Si} =$

$\dfrac{[30.97+(0.382)(10.81)][30.97+(2.618)(10.81)]}{(30.97+10.81)(28.09)} = 1.627 \approx \Phi$

We have: $\dfrac{[P+(1-\phi)B][P+(1+\Phi)B]}{(P+B)Si} \approx \Phi$

We know: $\dfrac{air}{H_2O} \approx \Phi$ and $\dfrac{P+B+Si}{C+N+O+H} \approx \Phi$

So, $\dfrac{[P+(1-\phi)B]\left[P+\left(1+\left(\dfrac{air}{H_2O}\right)\right)B\right]}{(P+B)Si} \approx \dfrac{P+B+Si}{C+N+O+H}$

Appendix

Let us say the geometric mean between a and c is b. That is written: $b=\sqrt{ac}$. It is the length of a side of a square, b, that has the same area as a rectangle with sides a and c. To demonstrate this physically, let us take the geometric mean between 4 and 9. Four times nine is a rectangle with area 36. That corresponds to a square with side lenghts $6 = \sqrt{36}$:

In both instances we

have 36 squares

*In contrast the arithmetic mean, b, between to extremes a and c,
is $b=\dfrac{a+c}{2}$, is the midpoint b between a and c. Let us do this*

for a=2 and b=8. $5=\dfrac{2+8}{2}=\dfrac{10}{2}$:

```
  a    b    c
--2----5----8          b=midpoint between a and c.
```

The harmonic mean is the value that occurs the most in a set of values and, is given by:

$$b=\frac{2ac}{a+c}$$

Let us divide a line with length a into two parts

such that a=b+c and $\dfrac{a}{b}=\dfrac{b}{c}$:

```
|------------ a-----------------|
                |-----c-----|
|--------b----------|
------------------------------
```

$a=b+c$ *and* $\dfrac{a}{b}=\dfrac{b}{c}$ *combine as:*

$\left(\dfrac{a}{b}\right)^2-\dfrac{a}{b}-1=0$ *which can be solved*

for $\dfrac{a}{b}$ *by completing the square.*

$\dfrac{a}{b}$ *is the golden ratio denoted* Φ.

If we add the square of one half

the coefficient of $\dfrac{a}{b}$, *which is* $\dfrac{1}{4}$,

to both sides of the equation, it becomes:

$\left(\dfrac{a}{b}\right)^2-\dfrac{a}{b}+\dfrac{1}{4}=1+\dfrac{1}{4}$ *which is,*

$\left(\dfrac{a}{b}\right)^2-\dfrac{a}{b}+\dfrac{1}{4}=\dfrac{5}{4}$ *and factoring:*

$\left(\dfrac{a}{b}-\dfrac{1}{2}\right)^2=\dfrac{5}{4}$ *This has the solution*

$\dfrac{a}{b}=\Phi=\dfrac{\sqrt{5}+1}{2}\approx1.618$

The Author

www.ingramcontent.com/pod-product-compliance
Lightning Source LLC
Chambersburg PA
CBHW051216050326
40689CB00008B/1327